The
SPUR BOOK
of
PARALLEL SKI-ING

Also in the
SPURBOOK VENTURE GUIDE SERIES:

By Brown and Hunter:

In Preparation:

SPUR FOOTPATH GUIDES INCLUDE:

The
SPUR BOOK
of
PARALLEL SKI-ING

by
Terry Brown and Rob Hunter

SPURBOOKS LIMITED

Published by
Spurbooks Ltd.
6 Parade Court
Bourne End
Bucks

The authors would like to acknowledge the help of the Ski-schools at Les Arcs and Avoriaz, Haute-Savoie, France, and the Instructors of Les Ecoles des Ski, La Mongie and Cauterets, in the French Pyrenees.

ISBN 0 904978 82 6

Printed in England by Maund & Irvine Ltd., Tring, Herts.

CONTENTS

Page No.

INTRODUCTION

ABOUT THIS SERIES

Venture Guides fall into two broad categories. The first attempts to provide all outdoor enthusiasts, of any age and both sexes, with the basic skills all outdoor people should possess. They cover, therefore, such subjects as Knot Tying and Splicing, Map Reading and Compass Work, Camping Skills, First Aid, Weather Lore, and Survival and Rescue Techniques. Further titles, notably one on Swimming and Diving will follow.

The second category covers Venture Sports, that is, outdoor activities which are not team games. This section includes Sailing, Snorkelling, Basic Downhill Ski-ing, Backpacking, Hill-Trekking, Rock Climbing, Cross-Country Ski-ing, and now, Parallel Ski-ing.

ABOUT THIS BOOK

Every downhill ski-er, from the first moment he or she looks up a 'piste', before the would-be ski-er even puts the skis **on,** wants, above all, to ski parallel.

Those graceful controlled turns, the magic way the expert shifts direction, coming straight down those fearsome slopes, sailing over the 'moguls', all excite the envy and determination of the new ski-er.

This book has just one aim, to teach you, on your own or with a friend, to advance from the basic stages of the stem-turn, until you can parallel ski on moderate slopes with skill and confidence.

It breaks down the steps involved and gives advice on the practice necessary and the time you should devote to it. We assume nothing, and show errors as well as expertise.

Good ski-ing, as you will quickly learn, is composed of a host of little things; of getting the details right. It is hard to concentrate on all the requirements when you are moving fast into a turn, so we have taken the steps one at a time. Don't move onto the second step until the first has become instinctive. Keep practising, and good ski-ing ! ! !

HOW TO USE THIS BOOK

This book is a guide to the **elements** of parallel ski-ing. To get maximum benefit from it, you must take the instructions one page at a time, building on your success at mastering one technique and tackling the causes of each difficulty, as they occur, until you get over them and the correct movement or position is adopted naturally. Study the sections before each practice, trying to grasp what you should do. If, during the session you can't, decide if the reason is that you are doing one of the things you shouldn't do. 'DO's and DON'T's are given for all sections.

The basics get constant attention to fix them firmly in your mind, and constant repetition is the basis of learning all instictive skills. This book, practice, and a growing confidence, will show you how to parallel ski.

Chapter 1

GETTING THE BASICS RIGHT

Why can't you parallel ski? What **exactly** is the problem? Others can do it, drat them, so why not you? That's the first question you must ask yourself, and your instructor, and be sure you get an answer from each. Let me give you a personal illustration.

After a day falling headlong down the slopes of Austria, very tired, and with all confidence gone, I asked my instructor which was the **biggest** mistake I'd made all day. He thought for a minute and said, **"Well Rob, I don't think getting up this morning was a very good idea!"**

Very funny! However, when pressed, we discussed my lack of fitness and fear of the fall-line, and the tendency to over-edge in the turn. My skis—at 210 cm, were too long, and so were my poles. I changed to 185 cm skis and had 10 cms cut off each pole.

By now incensed, I marched into the ski-shop and cornered the boot-expert. He tore off my boots and two pairs of thick socks, and my boot size fell from 11 to 9! I went to bed early, and decided that the stem-turn days were over. The next day I invested in some private lessons, and happily, I can now parallel ski.

Let's just think this story over, for there are lessons here.

Firstly, without good fitting boots, you won't be able to learn parallel ski-ing. You won't have the control. With the incorrect length of ski or over-long poles, you are just making difficulties for yourself. If you stay up all night or go ski-ing completely unfit, with weak legs, then steep mogul slopes will tire you before your technique develops sufficiently.

Finally, determination. You may, gentle reader, be a natural downhill, gung-ho, hot-rodder. In which case you have wasted the price of this book. However, if you are the normal timorous mortal who views awful drops with natural reservation, then you may prefer to stay on easy slopes and stick to gentle stems.

The problem is that with this you can't go very far. You must parallel to go high where the great ski trails are. Sooner or later, however much you dislike the prospect, you must point those skis down the slope and learn to parallel. So **determination** is an important factor whether you summon it early or late.

Finally, a word of comfort. Once you tackle steep slopes, they seem to flatten out. Fear, once tackled, ebbs away. It really is quite easy. All you have to do is try.

Fig. 1

BOOTS AND EQUIPMENT

You will have a head start if your equipment is the right size and correctly fitted. Advice on this is contained at length in our book on Basic Ski-ing, also in this series, but the basic requirements are as follows . . .

BOOTS

The most important piece of equipment is the boot. Boots transmit your intentions from the foot, through the binding, to the ski. With ill-fitting boots you will find ski-ing difficult, and probably very uncomfortable. Ill-fitting boots, which cause sore feet or ankles put more people off ski-ing than anything else, so:

GET GOOD FITTING BOOTS, WHATEVER YOU DO.

Change them again and again until they do fit, no matter how long it takes. 'Flow-fit' boots, which have a padded lining that adjusts to your foot when warm, are very suitable.

CHOOSING YOUR BOOTS

Get hold of a ski boot and examine it. Nowadays boots are made from plastic, have a hard outer shell, and a soft, padded, removable liner, a long tongue, and do up with clips. They are often hinged at the ankle. Examine your boots and clips carefully (Figure 1).

To get boots right, proceed as follows. (We assume a 4-clip boot).

1. Ask the assistant for your normal shoe size.

   Continental sizes are (approximately) as follows:

U.K.	6	7	8	9	10	11
Continental	38	40	42	43	44	45

   Whatever your **actual** size is doesn't matter. You want boots that **fit,** but by asking for your normal shoe size you get into the right size area. Wear your ski socks.

2. Undo the clips completely, and pull out the tongue towards the boot toe.

3. Put the foot into the boot endeavouring to press your heel back into the rear of the boot. 'Flow-fit' boots take time to warm up and adjust to your foot.

4. Fold back the tongue neatly, and do up the bottom clips, to grasp the foot firmly, but not tightly. Do the same with the top clip, leaving the middle one, if any, undone.

5. Stand up.

6. Your big toe is probably touching the front of the boot. Unless it is pressing hard enough to be uncomfortable, this is all right.

7. Now, keeping the heels of the boots on the ground, and looking down, flex the knees forward, over the toes of the boots. Your heels should now slip back into the heel of the boot, and your toes ease off the front. If this happens, the fit is probably all right. The toes should be able to wriggle.

8. Still keeping the knees flexed as far forward as possible, bend down or get a friend to do up the third clip, if any, as tightly as possible. this is the clip that clamps your heel into the rear of the boot, and keeps it there. For good ski-ing THE HEEL MUST NOT RISE—remember that. You probably now feel—what a rigmarole! Quite so, but comfortable, well-fitting boots can make or break your ski-ing,and make the difference between becoming a good ski-er and retiring miserably to the bar. So, read this section several times until you are certain you will know how to try on a pair of ski boots. They may feel very stiff and strange, like deep-sea divers' boots, but those are your feet in there, and only you can decide, from the above information, if you have a good fit.

Now for some final points:

(a) Most people wear boots that are TOO BIG. It's the most common fault, so watch out for it.

(b) Your own shoe size is only a guide. Get boots that fit, not your usual 8½.

(c) Ski boots are for ski-ing, not for walking. When you are not flexing, the toes should touch the front.

(d) When flexed, and clipped up, the heels should be held firmly down, the toes just off the front and the toes free to wriggle.

(e) We have assumed for this that your boots have four clips, but they can have any number. Just be sure that when the clips are done up **the heel does not rise.**

(f) The padded tongue fits comfortably over the shin.

Finally, again, if your boots don't fit, or are paining you, change them as often as it takes, until you solve the problem. The new boots may not rub you in the same place as the previous pairs.

LENGTH OF SKIS

For the last ten years, the trend of opinion has been for the ski length ski-ers' height ratio, to get less. People skied on ever shorter skis and this led, eventually, to the development of ski-evolutif.

At present the trend is reversing itself slightly, and long skis are becoming more fashionable again.

You must ski on skis that are right for you, and your height is only one, and the least important factor in the choice. It used to be held that the correct length was judged when you stood with your

11

STEP IN BINDING

PLATE BINDING

Fig. 2

12

hand over your head, and the correct length ski was the one where the tip fitted into the palm of the upheld hand. This would be a very long ski, by present standards, suitable only for cross-country ski-ing.

To get the right length of ski, consider:

1. Your height.
2. Your weight and build.
3. Your degree of fitness.
4. Your ski-ing experience and skill.

The taller, heavier, fitter and more experienced you are, the longer the ski. If you are a short, thin, asthmatic dart player, then your skis will be somewhat minute.

Study the lengths for men and women and, considering the points just covered, go for the longer or shorter length. The ski length, in centimetres, is cut into the side of the ski.

BINDINGS (Figure 2)
Bindings are a very critical piece of equipment, and the choice is wide. However, the beginner will usually have the choice made for him, and again, there are only two basic areas, not counting:

CABLE BINDINGS
If you are offered 'cable' bindings, refuse them. Pay more for better bindings if necessary. Get:

STEP-IN BINDINGS
The toe of the binding is usually fixed on a swivel, while the heel-plate rises. You put the boot toe into the toe of the binding, step down and the heel-plate clicks down and shut. To release, you usually depress a catch in the heel-plate. In a fall, with a 'step-in' binding, the toe releases sideways, and the heel-plate rises, to free the boat.

PLATE BINDINGS
With these the boot is fixed to a flat-plate and the plate in turn, is fixed to the ski. In a fall, the whole plate slips away from the ski. Plate-bindings, which allow the boot to release under any strain, are highly recommended. Their release qualities are superior to step-in or cable bindings.

ADJUSTING BINDINGS

The bindings should be tight enough to stay on for hard-ski-ing, and easy falls, but should come off at once if you take a real spill.

If you find your binding releasing while you are doing a snow plough turn, for example, then it is too loose. If you come a hard cropper and your skis stay on, then they are too tight, and may need to be eased. Most bindings have a dial or grid, which indicates where the correct fit (for your boots) should be. Note this as you leave the fitting bench, and if you see the mark has moved, check the binding, and have them adjusted if necessary. Bindings can freeze. If you take the skis off at lunchtime, snap the bindings a few times to free them before you put the skis on again, especially if the day is cold, foggy or icy.

CHECK YOUR BINDINGS

Toe, heel, and plate bindings should release, with difficulty. Try and move them, and if it's too easy, or impossible, have them adjusted.

POLES

Ski-sticks are more correctly known as poles.

The correct length of the pole is when you can hold it, tip sunk in snow, with the forearm at right angles to the body. The best way to judge this is to hold the pole upside down, by the spike below the basket. If the butt rests on the ground and the forearm is straight, the pole is the right length. Better a little short than too long, for parallel.

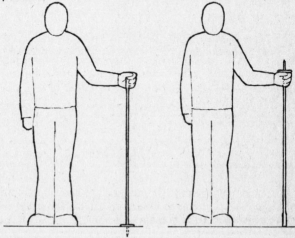

Fig. 3

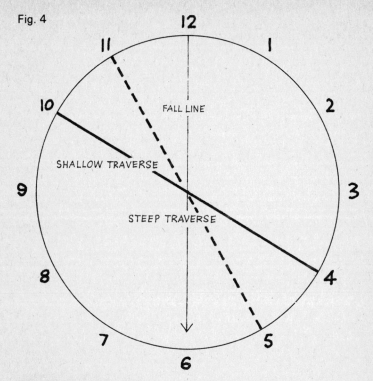

Fig. 4

FALL LINE

SHALLOW TRAVERSE

STEEP TRAVERSE

STARTING POINT

We are going to assume that you have some ski-ing experience, and can perform the following basic manoeuvres, which have been outlined in Basic Ski-ing: traversing, the snow plough turn, side-slipping etc. These elements, with others we are about to learn, will form part of your parallel turns.

Now you need a slope. Choose one with an angle of about 45°, as wide as possible, and with a good run out at the bottom. To give direction and traverse angle, we will use the "clock" system i.e. a shallow traverse, left to right, will be from 10 o'clock to 4 o'clock. A steep one would be from 11 o'clock to 5 o'clock.

FITNESS

Ski-ing is a sport. You will enjoy it more, find it easier, and be less tired, if you get fit, or at least fitter, before you go. If your idea of

15

exercise is getting out of bed in the morning, then your first few days on the slopes will prove a traumatic experience.

Getting fit is perhaps more important for the beginner than for the more experienced ski-er. The beginner uses fewer lifts, does more climbing on skis, and being inexperienced, puts unnecessary effort into his ski-ing.

You don't need bulging muscles, you need firm, flexible, supple ones. Get them used to being used, especially over the three weeks before you go. While it would be best for everyone if we exercised all the time, to get the best from your ski-ing, try and get fit by exercising your body in the three weeks before you go. Don't overdo it to begin with.

Chapter 2

THE STEM TURN

We are going to get the basics right, and the basic turn on a steep slope is the stem turn.

STARTING POSITION

Get into the traversing position, skis together, upper ski in front, weight on downhill ski, skis edged into the slope. Now:-

Point the skis MORE down the slope. However much you **want** to point them, however much you usually point them down, point them MORE. The turn will then be easier.

Hold the poles lightly, at shoulder width, and push off, looking straight ahead, and well across the slope, not just a few metres ahead. Look and think DOWNHILL. Face the fact of the slope and get used to it.

THE TURN (Fig. 5)

For the basic stem, you move from the traverse position as follows:

DO

1. Bend the knees.

2. Open out the uphill ski, to make a 'V' with the lower one.

3. Transfer your weight gradually on to the 'V'd uphill ski. You will start to turn downhill.

Now, this is the point where you formerly gave up, and sat down backwards, or fell over, out of the turn—DON'T: Instead:

DO

4. Lean forward, and look out of the turn.

By so doing, the turn will continue round and you will again be traversing the slope, weight on the now outer downhill ski.

DO

5. Slide the upper ski in to the traverse position.

6. Correct your traverse position and go STRAIGHT INTO ANOTHER TURN.

Now if you descend the slope, practising the stem, in a series of linked turns, for say one hour, you will, firstly, improve your stemming and secondly realise that it's still not quite right. The time has come for a few refinements.

TRANSFER THE
WEIGHT GRADUALLY
ONTO THE OUTSIDE
SKI

BEND THE KNEES
STEM OUT THE
UPHILL SKI

Fig. 5

START IN TRAVERSING POSITION.
UPPER SKI IN FRONT
WEIGHT ON DOWNHILL SKI

NOW
SLIDE THE
UPPER
SKI IN

COMMON ERRORS (Figs. 6 & 7)

Failing to **bend the knees** before the turn is a very common error, and one with woeful consequences. With bent knees, you can press out on the outer ski, and induce the turn, tightening it if necessary as you cross the fall-line. So, bend the knees.

But, and it's a big but, when pressing out for the turn, **never allow the outer leg to get straight,** with the knee locked. If you do, your weight will fall inward, and you will **either** over edge, with the inner edge of the outer ski hooking you round, or full back into the turn. Use your weight, not your muscle.

Turning with a stiff outside leg is a common and major fault. Keep the outer knee bent and the weight between the hips.

DO

Keep the body evenly between the skis, knees bent, pressing out the turn, and letting the weight drift across as you cross the fall-line.

Swinging the shoulders round when attempting to induce the turn is another common error, so,

DO

Keep the shoulders square, and keep the skis on the snow. This will give you a good gliding turn.

SPEED

You may find, when traversing the slope that, because of your steeper line, you are going too fast for comfort. Side-slip to lose speed, before straightening up for the turn. **Don't** stem out, after a side slip, with the tips pointing **uphill,** or you won't get round.

Now re-read this section on Errors, and carry on practising. Once the Stem has been perfected, you will be less worried about the fall-line, and ready for another turn. Spend at least one hour refining your traverse position, side slipping and stem turns. Take it in turns, each correct the other's error. **Never** do just one turn always do at least **three.**

GIVING ADVICE

Unless something is **very** wrong, don't shriek advice at your partner when he (she) is attempting a turn. They either won't hear you, or, distracted, in attempting to correct what they have just done they will get something else wrong. Discuss **major** errors after each attempt. If you get the major error corrected, many minor errors will cease to occur.

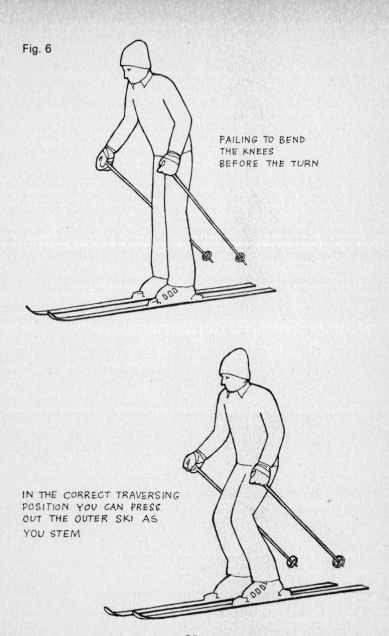

Fig. 6

FAILING TO BEND
THE KNEES
BEFORE THE TURN

IN THE CORRECT TRAVERSING
POSITION YOU CAN PRESS
OUT THE OUTER SKI AS
YOU STEM

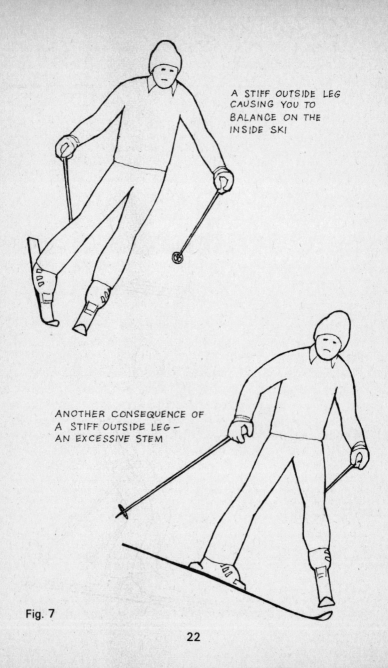

A STIFF OUTSIDE LEG
CAUSING YOU TO
BALANCE ON THE
INSIDE SKI

ANOTHER CONSEQUENCE OF
A STIFF OUTSIDE LEG —
AN EXCESSIVE STEM

Fig. 7

22

Chapter 3

UPHILL STOP CHRISTIES

So far, we have worked on perfecting the traverse and stem turn. This involves moving the uphill ski out to form a V. We must now start learning to turn with the skis together and the best way to learn is to turn UPHILL.

This turn is a useful step in the progressive learning of parallel ski-ing, for it involves more elements, and is also useful for increasing confidence, as it is a stopping movement, useful on the steepest slopes, where you may be afraid that, once under way, you cannot stop.

STARTING POSITION

This turn is easier on steeper slopes and with a steeper line. Get in the traverse position and head across the slope on a steep incline, 10 to 4, or better still 10 to 5 (see Fig. 4).

The turn:
1. Bend the knees.
2. Press the knees into the slope, thus edging the skis. Keep the skis together.
3. Keep facing down the slope.
4. Press out on the skis, **from the bend knees,** flattening them as you do so.
5. As the legs straighten you will turn up the slope, and stop.

Notice the importance of the bent knees at the start. If you do not bend the knees **before** the turn, you won't be able to press out on the skis, and round the turn out.

This turn should be practised **many times** at ever steeper angles.

COMMON ERRORS

The most common error is swinging the shoulders up the hill, to induce the turn.

Study the points given and the diagram (Fig. 8) and when turning, keep looking down the slope, pressing out the turn from the knees.

At this stage, don't induce the turn by planting the pole but concentrate on turning by flexing the legs and pressing out the turn, pushing the snow away from the underside of your skis.

PRESS KNEES
INTO THE SLOPE
EDGING THE SKIS

PRESS OUT
AND FLATTEN SKIS
UNWEIGHTING

Fig. 8

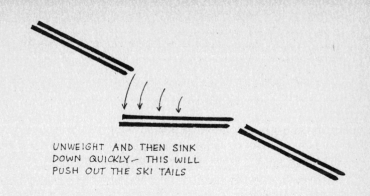

UNWEIGHT AND THEN SINK
DOWN QUICKLY — THIS WILL
PUSH OUT THE SKI TAILS

STOPPING AT SPEED

Your control and confidence will grow, if you intersperse the uphill stop-christies with skidded stop turns, commenced with a side slip.

Employ this turn when you feel the speed before the turn is excessive.

Drill:

1. From a steep traverse, flatten the skis into a side slip.
2. As the speed falls, bend the knees, lean forward and press the knees into the slope, and as the skis come round,
3. Keep the body facing downhill and come to a stop.

Please re-read this carefully, study the drawings and practise this manoeuvre many times, to right and left.

The turn involves:

1. Keeping the skis parallel.
2. Bending and flexing the knees.
3. Keeping the body facing downhill throughout the turn.
4. Pressing out the skis.

Item 2 will form the basis of the next chapter, when we learn the basics of unweighting the tails of the skis, an essential requirement for the parallel turn.

It is extremely important to keep the body mobile. Don't stand on your skis, stiff and erect. **Flex** and **bend,** through the turn.

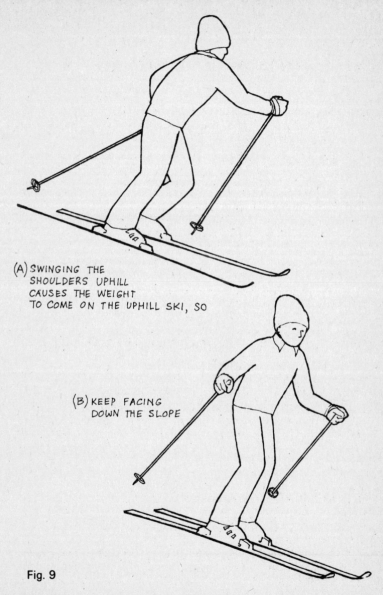

(A) SWINGING THE
SHOULDERS UPHILL
CAUSES THE WEIGHT
TO COME ON THE UPHILL SKI, SO

(B) KEEP FACING
DOWN THE SLOPE

Fig. 9

Chapter 4

UNWEIGHTING: FLEXING: EXTENSION

Good ski-ers ski well because they use their weight, balance and technique, to master the slopes at speed. The beginner finds it very difficult to control his skis, not because they are heavy and awkward, but because the ski-er has not learned to control them.

UNWEIGHTING (Fig. 10)

The boots hold the feet and the bindings link boot and ski. If you stand on the skis, and throw your weight from the bent knees up and forward, you will, momentarily, **unweight the tails of the** skis. Thus unweighted, they will easily turn, especially if un-weighting linked to a pole and leg movement.

This method of "unweighting" throwing the weight **up** and **forward** is called "upwards unweighting".

It is possible, and some say easier, to unweight the skis by the reverse method, "downward unweighting", and some who normally ski with an upright stance will find this more natural.

For "down unweighting", from the upright stance on the skis, let the knees flex while throwing the weight down and forward which also has the effect of **unweighting the tails of the skis.**

So find a steep slope and run a steep traverse (11 to 5) into an uphill stop christie, and let us practise the unweighting.

UPWARD UNWEIGHTING

Position: Keep the knees well bent, the weight forward, the hands forward at shoulder width. Don't be afraid to move fast, you know how to stop remember. THINK downhill.

Turn: Flexing the knees to give more spring, throw the weight forward and UP. Imagine your chest getting **over** the tips of your skis. Bend the knees into the slope, and you will skid round into the turn, the shoulders swinging out, to face down the slope. Press out the turn, and stop.

DOWNWARD UNWEIGHTING

Position: Adopt an upright stance, body loose and knees slightly bent. Ride across the slope easing out the bumps until you reach the turning spot.

The Turn: Bend the knees and throw the shoulders forward over the boots, to shift the weight from the tails to the tips of the skis. Bend the knees into the slope and skid round into the turn,

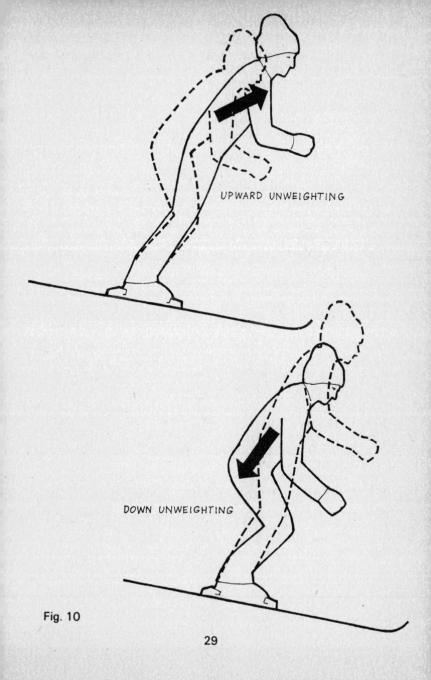

UPWARD UNWEIGHTING

DOWN UNWEIGHTING

Fig. 10

straightening the knees to press out the turn, and, stop as usual, facing down the slope.

Please note that these two methods have only one object: to unweight the skis and make it possible to turn them **together without stemming**.

Practice unweighting by both, or either method, for unweighting is essential to successful parallel ski-ing.

Flexing: The legs are the engines of the downhill ski-er, and they have to pump. Poor ski-ers don't use their legs. They simply stand on the skis and let the slope take control.

Let your legs drive you over the ground, flexing and extending, ironing out the shocks, driving the snow away from the base of the ski, and powering you into and through the turns.

Extension: The movement of the body, from the crouched traverse to the forward unweighted position, is called "extension". Extension, up and forward, will unweight your skis.

A Point to Remember: Many inexperienced ski-ers find flexing and extension difficult because either they don't understand why they are doing it, or are in the wrong position to begin with.

So remember: The object of flexing and extension is to unweight the skis, but you will be unable to flex or extend if you have already done so! Flexing and Extension are **movements, not positions.**

Unless you have a crouched traverse position **before** the turn, you will not be able to unweight during it, for unless you are **down,** you can't go **up.** If you are **up** you can't go **down**—got it?

If you are **up,** in an uphill stance, you can **only** use the downward unweighting.

Read this again—it is very important.

You must use your legs and body, in a continual flowing, flexing and extending movement.

Watch those experts and see how they flow down the slopes. It is the flexing and extending that gives that graceful line.

Chapter 5

THE STEM CHRISTIE

The stem christie is, for the great majority of holiday skiers, THE turn. Most skiers never get beyond this turn, and if they are to progress, then a perfect stem-christie is a necessary step.

STEM TURN AND STEM CHRISTIE (Fig. 11)

The stem-christie differs from the stem turn in many respects and, if you attempt a stem turn under certain conditions, it will speedily develop into a stem christie.

Compared with the stem turn, a stem christie is:

1. Faster.
2. Closer to the fall-line (10 or 11 to 5)

and

3. Has a smaller and shorter lasting stem.

Read this again. Then:

Starting position:

1. Traverse the slope, **at a steep angle to the fall-line**—running across towards **4** or **8,** then

DO

2. Flex the knees, lowering the body, upper ski in front, weight on downhill ski and . . .

DO

3. Stem out slightly and . . .

DO

4. Come up.

As you cross the fall-line, **bring the skis together.** By coming up at speed, you **will have unweighted the tails** and the movement will be easy. Once across the fall-line,

DO

5. Flex down and forward.

DO

6. Weight onto downhill ski, and press out to complete the turn.

DON'T

Make too wide a stem: You will either go into a plough, or fall out of the turn. (Fig. 9, Page 27).

CLOSE THE INNER SKI TO
THE OUTER SKI

Fig. 11

STEM OUT
SLIGHTLY

LOWER THE BODY AND
PLANT THE POLE

33

DON'T Lean into the Slope: This is caused by fear. If you are catching your inside edge, then you are leaning into the slope. Lean out. Keep the skis flat. Use your weight, don't carve away with those edges.

Fall Backwards: When you are on the fall-line, skis together, you speed up. This gives you a nasty moment, and you will either:

1. Fall over backwards, or

2. Stem out wildly, flinging your shoulders round and skid round to end up facing across or up the slope, skis ploughed. Are you doing this? (See Fig. 7. Page 22).

If so: your weight is wrong. You are leaning back (away from that slope) because you are afraid.

Your weight should, at this moment, be down and forward, evenly over the skis, the knees flexed, ready to press you out round in the turn. Finally, DON'T:

Fall Out of the Turn: As the turn steepens or just as you cross the fall-line, you catch the outside edge, and fall out across the outer ski.

This is usually caused by allowing the outer leg to get straight or by attempting to stem round the turn, rather than by using the weight and flexing.

DO

1. Keep the skis flat on the snow.

You can see the snag with perfecting the stem christie. There is a lot to do, and it all happens very quickly.

Notice, however, the basic points:

1. Steep angle to fall-line.

2. Down–up–down motion of the body into and through the turn.

3. **Slight** stem out, and weight transferred onto outer ski.

4. Look down the slope—always.

Now if you practise this, you will soon find that you are getting very fluid turns, and that the body movement gives you full freedom to turn the skis out.

COMMON PROBLEMS

Too much Speed: Speed helps you in the turn, but you can have too much of it. Control your speed by little slide slips while traversing, but go steeply into the turn—slowly if you must, but **steeply.**

Fear of the Fall-line: Start on even slopes, and find steeper ones as your skill and confidence develop. Fear of the fall-line is

THE SHOULDERS SHOULD BE ACROSS THE FALL LINE AS YOU CROSS IT AND ANGLED TO FACE DOWNHILL THROUGHOUT THE TURN

TURNING THE DOWNHILL SHOULDER UP THE SLOPE IS A COMMON ERROR

Fig. 12

very natural and common, but it must be overcome. Be aware that fear is your problem and face it. It is very noticeable how a skier's skill and confidence improves **after** a fall. It doesn't hurt, and, that out of the way, you can concentrate on tackling the errors.

COMMON ERRORS

1. Not bending the knees.

A very common error is to stem out, go round, into the fall-line with the skis apart, and then lift the inner ski over. Your outer leg is locked straight, and you are leaning in. It looks ungainly and it will result in a fall. Keep the skis close together, weight evenly between them, and slide the skis into line.

2. **Shoulders:** Keep your shoulders angled, across the skis, and across the slope. Your shoulders should be across the fall-line as you cross it, and angled to face downhill at all other times.

Common Errors: The common error is to try and turn the downhill shoulder UP the slope. In fact, you turn the uphill shoulder down the slope, and lead with it. Study the diagram (Fig. 12) and you will see how your shoulders should look.

Practice: The stem christie needs a lot of practice, and if you work on it for say half a day, descending slope after slope, time after time, getting each part right, one skier correcting the other after each series of linked turns, you will certainly improve.

Never do just one turn and stop. Do three. Then you will start on the opposite traverse. Read this chapter at least once before each full descent, and resolve to get another part refined, without forgetting the others, on each attempt.

This improved, if not perfected, you can proceed to the parallel turn itself.

Chapter 6

THE PARALLEL TURN

Pole Planting: At this level—beginning the parallel turn, the beginner is so anxious to go round with his skis together that he lets all else go hang. **DON'T.**

Also at this stage, the poles are used, and as their use is important to a successful parallel, we want you to understand that planting the poles correctly is an essential part of the parallel turn.

Read and observe the following points closely:

1. When heading into the turn, hold the arms slightly away from the body, elbows bent, and fists forward of the knees. The poles are slanted to the rear, baskets just behind the heels.

2. Approaching the turning point, swing the pole forward GENTLY from the WRIST.

3. **Plant the downhill pole vertically, by flexing the knees.**

Let us examine Point 3 more closely. Read it again. That is what you DO.

You DO NOT

1. Reach forward with the pole as if spearing a piece of paper. Or

2. Plant the pole by dropping the shoulder.

By flexing the knees as you plant the pole, you are putting yourself into the "ready to unweight" position—now do you see the idea?

If you find this difficult, a good tip, especially on steep slopes, is to ski with **very** short poles. This forces you to bend the knees just to get the pole in, and, even more important, reminds you that flexing is necessary.

3. Plant the pole vertically, about midway between the boot toe and the ski-tip. This spot will vary according to your height, but that is the general area.

So, once again:

1. Hold the poles gently to the rear while traversing.

2. Swing the downhill pole forward from the WRIST until vertical.

3. Plant the pole by flexing the knees, midway between boot and ski tip.

We now have you at the turning spot, angled steeply to the fall-line, flexed and with the pole planted.

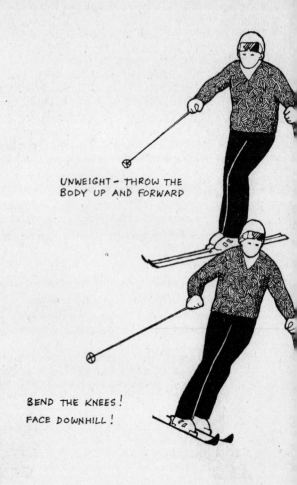

UNWEIGHT — THROW THE
BODY UP AND FORWARD

BEND THE KNEES!
FACE DOWNHILL!

Fig. 13

PLANT THE POLE BY
FLEXING THE KNEES

TAKE A STEEP LINE

DOWN AGAIN READY FOR
ANOTHER TURN

TRAVERSE

What do you do now?

UNWEIGHT—UNWEIGHT—UNWEIGHT!

1. Throw the body from the chest up and forward, flexing the downhill wrist.
2. Round you go. Keep the skis together and flat on the snow.
3. As you go round:
   1. Lean out and face downhill.
   2. Bend the knees flexing down, weight now on the downhill ski.
   3. Press down with the heels, hips into the hill, to side-slip if necessary. Traverse position again. Keep going, and straight into another turn.

DON'T (Fig. 14)

1. Stem the outer ski.
2. Lift the inner ski off the snow and step round.
3. Let the hips come forward.
4. Let the downhill shoulder lead.
5. Let the outer leg get stiff and locked.
6. Lean back.

DO

1. Think DOWNHILL—not a few metres ahead but for the bottom of the slope. Unweight positively—not feebly, and,
2. Keep the body loose and flexing.
3. Keep the skis on the snow.
4. Keep the weight between the skis.
5. Do more than one turn, do, or attempt to do at least **three** linked turns, never push out and stop.
6. Keep at it.

The parallel turn is like riding a bike. There is a knack to it, with lots of do's and dont's and it depends, like riding a bike, on weight, speed and confidence.

How to practise: Find a slope or part of the piste, that is at least 25% steeper than you like. Go to the top and note three turning points in the slope, at 5 o'clock, 8 o'clock and 5 o'clock repeating in a line, one to another down the slope.

Look DOWN the slope. You are going to go DOWN, not across or to and from, but DOWN.

Fig. 14

DO NOT REACH FORWARD WITH THE POLE OR DROP THE SHOULDER

DO NOT STEM THE OUTER SKI

DO NOT LEAN BACK

DO NOT LEAD WITH THE DOWNHILL SHOULDER

If you can, it is sometimes better to mark the turning points with twigs, or slalom poles, or even spare clothing. This gives you a definite point to turn round, and can be helpful.

Read the sections on the turn carefully, and make your run, through three turns at least, without stopping.

Concentrate on the Major points:

1. Planting the pole correctly, flexing.

2. **Unweighting.**

3. Skis together.

4. Looking downhill.

Get the major points right and many smaller ones will be overcome at the same time. Get your friends to comment on the points of your turns, good as well as bad.

Then let them descend, and by observing and commenting on their errors and noting their good points, the elements of the turn will start to break down, to you as well.

SPEED

The parallel turn is a fast turn. You may find, initially, that even though you don't like the slope or the speed, you need speed to get round.

This is due to poor unweighting techniques. As you practise and as your fear is overcome, you will notice that you **seem** to be turning more slowly.

Actually, you are overcoming the fear of the slope and your brain is adapting to the manoeuvre. Once this starts, you will be able to refine the turn, correcting all the little details.

You will also be able to parallel on shallower traverses, since your improved technique will enable you to swing the skis through a wider arc.

Chapter 7

PARALLEL EXERCISES

As you will have realised, parallel ski-ing is not so easy and needs a certain dexterity. It requires, apart from specific technique, precise movements of the skis, the legs and the body.

Each little skill you acquire will help your control and increase your confidence. The following exercises can be tried if you cannot seem to master a complete turn, no matter how you try. They can be employed, just for practice or fun, by ski-ers of quite moderate ability. The exercises break down the basic elements of parallel turns.

Tail Hopping: Unweighting the tails of the skis is an essential part of parallel ski-ing.

To practise tail-hopping, run an even traverse, on the 4 or 8 o'clock line, and

1. Flex the knees, lean forward.
2. Throw the weight up and forward, and
3. Hop up, the heels of the skis clear of the ground.
4. After each hop, flex the knees and crouch.
5. Repeat.

Run several traverses, hopping as high and as often you can, flexing afterwards. If your heels are lifting and your skis are on the snow, tighten your clips or get smaller boots. Remember you must flex if you want to extend. So flex-up-flex-up-flex-up—and keep it going.

Tail Hopping on the Fall-line: This is the same exercise as the one above, but done directly down the fall-line. Look at the bottom of the slope, and try and throw the weight up and forward **from the chest**. Always sink into a forward flexed position after each hop. If you don't do this, you won't be able to hop—you can't go **up** if you already **are** up.

Pole Planting with Flexing: Run a traverse, or down the fall-line, under the eye of a critical friend, watching for correct pole planting technique.

1. Start in a fairly upright stance, poles slanted to the rear.
2. Swing the poles forward, and plant them vertically BY FLEXING the knees—NOT by dropping the shoulders. Do not let the pole go forward from the vertical line.
3. Repeat across or down the slope and keeping practising.

Slalom: Competition is a great spur. If you get the chance to enter the Friday races,. do so. If slalom poles are left on the slopes, by running a course through them, your turns will tighten up remarkably, and equally important, unless you get it right, you won't make the next gate. So try slaloming at any opportunity.

Fear: Knowledge dispels fear. That is the motto of the Parachute School. Think about what you are doing and dispel fear of the slopes or speed, by concentrating on what you are doing.

Just for the record, my instructor overcame my own, fairly well engrained fear of heights and steep slopes by a direct and somewhat brutal method.

After about half an hour, he stopped and said "You are afraid". "Fear is making you a bad ski-er". (It sounded better in French).

FLEX THE KNEES
LEAN FORWARD

THROW THE WEIGHT
UP AND FORWARD
HOP THE SKI TAILS
CLEAR OF THE SNOW

TAIL HOPPING

Fig. 15

He then proceeded to send me down terrible slopes, straight schuss. It was quite nasty, and the descent was made at speeds where to fall would be even nastier, so somehow or other I stayed on my feet. After spending the rest of the morning going down one steep slope after another, I was exhausted, but no longer scared. I don't recommend this method, but if all else fails, you might care to try it.

FIG. 16

Pole Planting with Tail Hopping: Link the above two exercises into one, first across the slope, then down the fall-line. If you slightly "over-cook" a hop on the fall-line, you will be into a 'wedel', so let it happen and keep it up as long as you can.

Flexing and Unweighting: This is a very beneficial exercise, on the schuss or traverse.

From an upright stance, unweight **up** and flex **down;** Up, down flex, up, down flex.

REPEAT

45

SWING THE POLE FORWARD
AND PLANT BY FLEXING
THE KNEES

POLE PLANTING AND TAIL HOPPING

FIG. 17

Side Hopping: This is the last exercise you can reasonably do, without going into a full turn.

Running a traverse, you can hop up, trying to land the ski tail above or below your pre-hop breakpoint.

Since this is an awkward manoeuvre it has useful training advantages.

To stay upright, you will have to flex, or edge, or flatten the skis quickly on landing. This will make you nimble and responsive to the results of your actions.

PLANT THE POLE
VERTICALLY WITH THE
FOREARM PARALLEL
TO THE SNOW

REPEAT

Fig. 16

Fig. 17

SIDE HOPPING

SHORT CUTS

Personally, I am not sure that there are any real short cuts. You need to know what you have to do, and go out and practice until you can do it. Private lessons will help, and can be recommended.

Chapter 8

MOGULS

Moguls are bumps. Big, uneven craters, and mounds carved on open slopes by the action of turning ski-ers. Most new and intermediate ski-ers dislike moguls, especially on the steep slopes of 45° or over. However, moguls are a fact of life on the ski-slope, so you must be able to tackle them.

First, try and realise that if tackled correctly, moguls make turning easier. To use them you just obey two simple rules.

1. Turn on the top of the mogul.
2. Keep turning.

Fig. 18

FLEXING THE KNEES TO ABSORB BUMPS.   Fig. 19

Most moguls are on several descent lines. Although they look like a confused jumble of hillocks, there is a path through them, so find and use it. Do **not** traverse woefully up and down across the slope, looking for a flat bit. Come up on a mogul and TURN, down, up on a mogul and TURN.

The point is, that on top of a mogul your ski tips and tails are free, and only the centre, under your weight, is in contact with the snow. Turning is much easier as there is less resistance, for the tails are free to turn.

THE MOGUL TURN

Turning on moguls does require a certain technique. The three turn points have been mentioned but are worth repeating.

1. Don't be afraid.

2. Turn on the top.

3. Keep turning.

Let us study the mogul turns in a typical situation. You have come down the piste through the trees, and arrived at the top right hand corner (looking down) of a well-moguled slope. You stop and quail. Others come bombing past you and lead out onto the slope. Study their routes and note the turning points.

The first turn on a mogul slope is always the most difficult. On the other hand, the spot to make it is usually the most obvious.

Traverse to the selected mogul, in the following position.

1. Skis slightly but not too far apart. You want good balance, but you **don't** want one ski either side of the mogul.

2. Weight evenly between the skis, **not** over the downhill one.

3. Lean well forward, and

4. Adopt a well flexed, knees-bent position.

Fig. 20

Ride out the bumps, flexing the knees and body as you rise and fall.

As you reach the turning point (the top of the mogul) your impetus and the upward pull will help unweight you forward. You now need to turn.

Planting the Pole: Plant the pole **down the side of the mogul,** level with your boot, and put some weight on it. This locks the shoulder down, at the turning point

The Turn: You are now riding up on the mogul, heading forward, both your shoulders are turning round the planted pole. You need to feel that you are swooping into the hollow.

Steer the ski tips down the mogul on the pole side, keeping the skis flat. Face down and out. This will swoop you right round into the hollow at the side of the mogul, and ready to traverse and turn on another one.

What you have done is this, you rode up onto the top of the lump, planted the pole, while flexed, unweighted forward and turned, slid down the side of the mogul and traversed away. It sounds easy if you say it quick!

That is the essence of the turn, but there are, as always, a few do's and dont's.

DO

1. Head downhill.
2. Turn quickly, after planting the pole on the side of the mogul.
3. Keep turning.
4. Turn on the top.
5. Keep flexed and lean forward.

DON'T

1. Lean backwards.
2. Plant the pole on top of the mogul—plant it **on the side.**
3. Let the legs get rigid, let them flex like a bed spring.
4. Let the ski tips cross.

SPEED

If you go too fast into moguls you can fly into the air. Keep some speed on, but control it by running up the side of moguls and side-

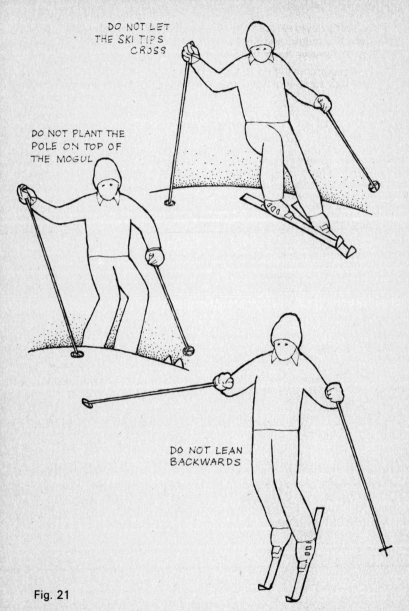

DO NOT LET
THE SKI TIPS
CROSS

DO NOT PLANT THE
POLE ON TOP OF
THE MOGUL

DO NOT LEAN
BACKWARDS

Fig. 21

53

slipping down to lose speed. When you have turned, edge the skis into the mogul and press out the turn. Aim for tight controlled turns, always heading downhill, and always turning.

Keep practising on mogul slopes. On the steep slopes, moguls are like steps in a staircase. They help you get down safely.

Chapter 9

JET TURNS, AVALEMENT, WEDEL

THE JET-TURN

The jet turn sounds terrific, and the person who named it deserves a medal, if only for making people nervous. However, it is a useful turn, an extension of the parallel, and especially useful if you get out of control on running moguls, or have to run down a slope, moguled or not, which is too narrow for an adequate traverse.

The two basic requirements for the jet turn are:

1. A backward-leaning, sitting down position.
2. The thrusting forward of the flattened parallel skis, across the fall-line.

The jet-turn is induced by the following action:

1. Checking the slide by edging, and
2. Initiating the turn by turning the upper body, always keep the upper body across the fall-line.

What you are doing is slamming the skis across the slope in a braking movement, and turning by rebounding from the check thus induced.

To learn the Turn: Once you have a fair grasp of the parallel turn, find an even slope, and one that is, to your now practised eye, quite easy.

Head down or close to the fall-line, in a schuss, knees bent and weight well forward. Plant the pole, and as your legs pass the planted pole **shoot the legs forward,** and swing the skis into a turn **across the fall-line.** You will be leaning well back, on your pole, but as the pressure on the skis slows your momentum, your own weight brings you up and forward.

Repeat this movement to the other side and continue on down the slope. As you can see, for checking speed on a fast slope, the "jet turn" is a useful manoeuvre.

Now study the diagram (Fig. 22) on the two following pages, and then go out and run through the turn as fast as possible. Tried slowly it won't work.

SIDE SLIP
TAILS OF
SKIS

BEND FORWARD
PLANT THE POLE DOWNHILL
AND SUPPORT YOURSELF ON IT

Fig. 22

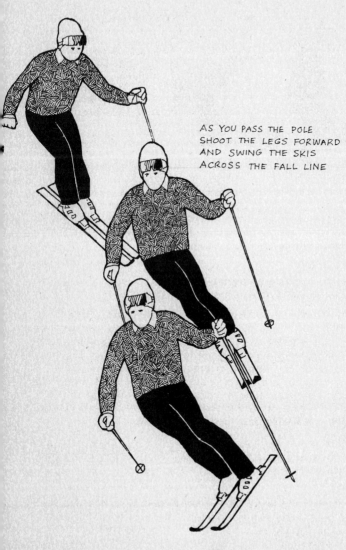

AS YOU PASS THE POLE
SHOOT THE LEGS FORWARD
AND SWING THE SKIS
ACROSS THE FALL LINE

AVALEMENT

A stage further on, lies the turn the French call 'avalement', which is best employed by the rapidly improving intermediate skier, rather than the adequate beginner, for avalement is used to turn full speed among moguls. You need speed, and good flex since the avalement turn cannot be done without it.

How to Start:

1. Run a fairly straight traverse across the slope, and look for a big mogul slightly above (not below) your line.

2. Plant the **uphill** pole, to climb up this uphill mogul, knees well flexed.

3. Once on top, follow through with the downhill pole, planted as for a mogul turn on the downhill side, extend (Fig. 23), and swoop down into the dip. You are flexing and extending up and over the hump, thus ironing it out. This will be a tight turn and you can fall out of it unless you flex the knees and edge the skis during the turn, flattening them as you point them down the mogul, and flexing down for the next turn.

DO NOT

Plant the pole on top of the mogul. This gives you a turn, but sends you back on your tracks.

DO

Keep flexing the legs to absorb the bumps. With flexed knees you can push away at the snow to control your turn and speed. With locked straight legs, half your control is gone.

NOTICE HOW THE SKIER MAINTAINS
THE SAME HEIGHT ACROSS
THE MOGUL

Fig. 23

WEDEL

A few years ago wedel was all the rage among intermediate and advanced skiers. People claimed to be doing wedel when they were doing all sorts of things, so let us start by defining wedel. Firstly, wedel is more than a turn. It is a method of descending a long even slope at speed and under control. In true wedel, your axis of descent is the fall-line, and **your ski tips stay on it.** Secondly, you **never** edge, or stem.

Since for true wedel, most methods of inducing a turn are discarded, how **do** you turn?

The method is called **counter-rotation,** ski tips facing one way, shoulders the opposite, and it works as follows:

1. Find an open, even, gentle slope.

2. Schuss directly down the fall-line, legs moderately flexed.

3. The arms are held out in front, fists at waist height.

4. Plant the pole, and swing the **tails** of the skis out across the fall-line, press out with the heels, this will check you.

5. While 4 is happening to the skis, swing the shoulders back at right angles to the fall-line and plant the pole again.

6. Plant the pole and swing the **tails** of the skis out across the fall-line, press out with the heels, this will check you, and repeat, repeat, repeat.

What you are after is a series of rythamic even swings and checks as close to the fall-line as possible.

These two turns Jet and avalement, and wedel, all take practice. They are refinements of parallel ski-ing and practicing them will improve your overall technique.

Fig. 24

Chapter 10

AIDS TO PARALLELING

SKI-EVOLUTIF

It would be impossible to conclude a book on parallel ski-ing without including a chapter on ski-evolutif, a process designed entirely to teach the beginner to parallel.

Many ski-ers believe that once you have learnt to induce a turn by stemming, you will continue to do so, however much you try not to, and never do a pure parallel turn. The short ski, evolutif, or GLM method attempts to overcome this by proceeding straight to paralleling, and avoids such techniques as the snow plough turn, and the stem.

Most Alpine resorts offer ski-evolutif, and the method is quite simple. You start on the first day with skis about one metre long, and learn the parallel swing. As your course proceeds, so your ski length increases.

The method is geared directly to the equipment and cannot be fully demonstrated here. It is much easier to turn on short skis, and once the techniques are grasped, it can be applied as the skis are lengthened.

So, if you get the chance to START ski-ing on the ski-evolutif method, then we recommend you do so.

However, if you are into your second or third season and just about to grasp the parallel turn, then we think you should not change skis in mid-piste, but work to refine and improve your technique.

There are, in practice, two snags. Firstly, ski-evolutif is not available everywhere, and secondly, many ski shops are becoming reluctant to swap a whole classful of skis over every couple of days, as the class itself improves.

However, there is no doubt that evolutif works. If you can find it, take it. Even take private lessons on evolutif skis, and then apply the techniques on your normal skis, when practising later.

However, the recreational skier's holiday is of limited duration, and if any method can be found to hasten the advancement of his ski-ing ability, then it is worth trying.

1. **Artificial Ski-ing:** In the U.K. there are over 90 artificial ski slopes distributed all over the country. There is a ski syllabus for all grades of skiers, and most slopes offer a parallel ski course of between 4 and 6 hours instruction.

    Taken in the weeks immediately preceeding your holiday,

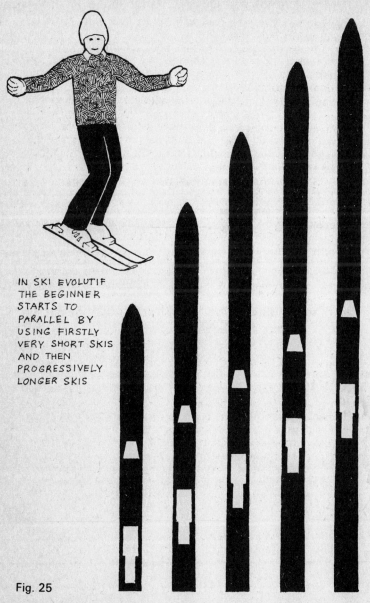

IN SKI EVOLUTIF
THE BEGINNER
STARTS TO
PARALLEL BY
USING FIRSTLY
VERY SHORT SKIS
AND THEN
PROGRESSIVELY
LONGER SKIS

Fig. 25

they can help you get a grasp of the principles, although there are certain differences.

Planting the pole for example, is difficult and we recommend the use of a shorter pole to aid flexing. Such minor points apart, if there is an artificial slope near you, go and use it.

2. **Private Lessons:** Once you are above the basic beginner stage, private lessons are well worthwhile. Try and go in the morning before lessons start and before you are too tired, rather than at the end of the day. Private lessons are not cheap, but if you love ski-ing and want to get better at it, they are well worth the money.

Finally, even when you have become an adequate parallel ski-er, never neglect the basics. Concentrate always on refining your techniques, and learn to cope with the endless variations in snow conditions, crust, ice, powder, or the deep heavy stuff—at least by now you are off the nursery slopes and the mountains are open to you—and good luck!